Recipes and styling by Valéry Drouet
Photographs by Pierre-Louis Viel

VALÉRY DROUET AND PIERRE-LOUIS VIEL

BURGERS

[BAGELS AND HOT DOGS]

h.f.ullmann

PREFACE!

Whether you enjoy them as a quick snack or a full meal with friends—burgers, bagels, and hot dogs can be continually reinvented and brought to life as versatile dishes in their own right. And no matter whether the occasion is elegant or more informal, two basics always apply: burgers are luscious, and they turn food into a feast.

Savory burgers made with beef carpaccio and broiled vegetables, with crispy chicken, with shrimp Thai-style, with smoked duck, and with goat cheese, or a sweet version made with a scrumptious chocolate filling... even the most reluctant connoisseurs, who tend to associate them—wrongly—with junk food, will come back for second helpings! The secret of good burgers lies in fresh ingredients and good-quality homemade sauces (see recipes on pp. 16–17.)

If you have time, make your own burger buns (see recipes on pp. 12–13); shape them individually, and flavor the dough with colorful spices or herbs. Then add your own touch by scattering them with seeds: sesame, poppy...

Alternatively, use store-bought buns (found in the bakery section of all supermarkets) or specialty breads, which are widely available and just as good. You can also ask your baker to create custom-made rolls, according to taste.

In every case, your friends will be amazed when offered these delicious sandwiches along with slices of skillet potato cake, Cajun spiced potatoes, or coleslaw with golden raisins (see recipes on pp. 20–21.)

Enjoy your burgers!

Valéry Drouet

CONTENTS!

CHICKEN, LAMB, ETC!

HOT DOGS & BAGELS!

SWEET BURGERS!

FISH & VEGETABLES!

ROLLS & BUNS!

WITH GRUYÈRE CHEESE

WITH BACON

WITH OLIVES

WITH CURRY

WITH CHORIZO SAUSAGE

WITH CAMEMBERT CHEESE

PLAIN WITH PUMPKIN
SEEDS

WITH SQUID INK
AND POPPY SEEDS

WITH CURRY AND
SESAME SEEDS

PLAIN WITH SESAME
SEEDS

WITH PAPRIKA

WITH SUN-DRIED
TOMATOES

TRADITIONAL ROLLS

Makes 6

For the dough:
2¾ cups (400 g) all-purpose flour
1 cup (250 ml) lukewarm water
1½ tsp (8 g) salt
2 tsp (8 g) dry yeast

For the flavorings (one of any of the following):
⅔ cup (80 g) olives, coarsely chopped
3½ oz (100 g) diced bacon, fried in a skillet until golden
¾ cup (80 g) grated Gruyère cheese
4 oz (120 g) Camembert cheese, diced
3½ oz (100 g) chorizo sausage, coarsely chopped
scant ½ cup (80 g) sun-dried tomatoes, coarsely chopped
⅔ cup (80 g) finely chopped walnuts
4 tsp (10 g) curry powder

For the toppings (one of any of the following):
2 tbsp (15 g) mixed seeds, e.g. caraway, cumin, aniseed, sesame, poppy
1 egg yolk

≫ Make the dough: in a food processor, mix together the flour, water, salt, and yeast. Knead the dough with the dough hook at low speed, for 5 minutes, then increase the speed slightly and let the machine run for 8–10 minutes. Add the flavoring of your choice.

≫ Make 6 rolls and lay them on a cutting board. Using a brush, coat the rolls with egg white diluted with a little water and sprinkle the seeds of your choice over the tops. Let the dough prove for 30–45 minutes at room temperature.

≫ Preheat the oven to 410 °F (210 °C) and place a small bowl of water inside.

≫ Put the rolls in the oven and bake for 15–20 minutes.

≫ Allow to cool, then carefully cut them in half to fill.

- Shape your rolls as required (into rounds, rectangles, or squares); you will then mold your meat accordingly.
- Toast the rolls, cut in half, before assembling the burger: they will taste better that way.
- Buy hot dog rolls, bagels, ciabatta, or milk rolls, or order them from your baker.

SPECIAL BURGER BUNS

Makes 6

For the dough:
3½ cups (500 g) all-purpose flour
1¼ cups (300 ml) lukewarm water
2 tsp (10 g) salt
2 tbsp (25 g) dry yeast
2 generous tbsp (35 g) softened butter

To color and flavor the dough (to taste):
- For black buns: generous 1 tbsp (15–20 ml) squid ink (available from the fresh fish counter)
- For yellow buns: 1 tsp (2.5 g) turmeric or curry powder
- For red buns: 1 tbsp (7.5 g) paprika or generous ½ cup (100 g) sun-dried tomatoes, chopped into small dice, or a generous pinch of cayenne.

For the topping (to taste):
- 2 tbsp (15 g) mixed seeds: sesame (white or black), poppy, nigella, pumpkin, linseeds, paprika, cumin, caraway...

≫ Make the dough: in a food processor, mix together the flour, water, salt, yeast, and butter. Add your chosen ingredient if you wish to flavor or color the dough. Knead the dough with the dough hook, at low speed, for 5 minutes, then increase the speed slightly and let the machine run for 8–10 minutes. Add the garnish of your choice. Let the dough rest for 30 minutes in the bowl.

≫ Make 6 buns and lay them on a cutting board. Sprinkle the seeds of your choice over the tops and let the dough prove for a further 45 minutes at room temperature.

≫ Preheat the oven to 410 °F (210 °C) and place a small bowl of water inside.

≫ Put the buns in the oven and bake for 15 minutes.

≫ Allow to cool, then carefully cut them in half to fill.

13

SAUCES!

KETCHUP

HOMEMADE
MAYONNAISE

WHITE SAUCE WITH HERBS

CHILI SAUCE

CURRY SAUCE

BÉARNAISE SAUCE

WHITE SAUCE WITH HERBS

- ½ cup (120 g) sour cream or Greek yogurt
- 2 tbsp (30 g) mayonnaise
- 1 bunch chives, finely chopped
- 1 clove garlic, finely chopped
- 1 shallot, finely chopped
- pinch of cayenne
- salt, milled pepper

》 In a bowl, mix together the sour cream and mayonnaise. Add the chives, garlic, shallot, and cayenne. Season with salt and pepper and stir. Store in the refrigerator.

KETCHUP

- Generous 1 lb (500 g) fresh tomatoes, very ripe
- 7 tbsp (100 g) superfine sugar
- 7 tbsp (100 ml) wine vinegar
- 1 onion, finely chopped
- 1 clove garlic, finely chopped
- pinch of mild chili powder
- salt, milled pepper

》 Wash the tomatoes, seed them, and chop into small pieces. Transfer to a large saucepan. Add the sugar, vinegar, onion, garlic, chili powder, salt, and pepper. Cook over low heat for 1½–2 hours, stirring occasionally.

》 Pass the sauce through a strainer. Allow to cool.

HOMEMADE MAYONNAISE

- 1 egg yolk
- generous 1 tbsp (20 g) prepared mustard
- generous ¾ cup (200 ml) vegetable oil
- 1 tbsp (15 ml) wine vinegar
- salt, milled pepper

》 Mix the egg yolk and the mustard together in a bowl. Gradually add the oil in a very thin stream, whisking constantly. Season with salt and pepper.

》 Stir in the wine vinegar at the end.

Use this mayonnaise as the basis to create your own sauces!

To make spiced ketchup, add ½ seeded chile pepper or 2 tbsp Tabasco® sauce to the mixture in the saucepan.

CURRY SAUCE

- ⅔ cup (150 g) mayonnaise
- 1 tsp (2.5 g) curry powder
- 1 tbsp (15 g) curry paste
- 2 tbsp (30 ml) lemon juice
- 1 small bunch cilantro (optional)

» In a bowl, mix together the mayonnaise and the curry powder. Add the curry paste and the lemon juice. Just before serving, mix in the freshly chopped cilantro. Store in the refrigerator.

CHILI SAUCE

- 2 shallots, finely chopped
- 1 red bell pepper, seeded and chopped
- 6 tbsp (100 g) ketchup
- 3 tbsp (45 ml) soy sauce
- 2 tbsp (30 ml) whiskey
- scant 2 tbsp (25 g) brown sugar

» Place the shallots and bell pepper in a large saucepan. Add the ketchup and the other ingredients. Stir, then cook over moderate heat for 10 minutes. Mix well. Allow to cool.

BÉARNAISE SAUCE

- generous 1 cup (250 g) butter, cut into small cubes
- ½ cup (60 g) shallots, finely chopped
- 1 tsp (2.5 g) coarsely milled white pepper
- 2 tbsp (10 g) freshly chopped tarragon
- ⅔ cup (150 ml) white wine vinegar
- 4 egg yolks
- salt, milled pepper

» Melt the butter in a double saucepan for 15–20 minutes over low heat without stirring. Using a skimmer, remove the white-colored impurities (i.e. casein and whey) which will float up to the surface, in order to obtain a clarified butter.

» Place the shallots, pepper, 1 tbsp tarragon, and vinegar in a saucepan and boil until the vinegar has evaporated. Remove from the heat; add the egg yolks and 2 tbsp cold water. Whisk over low heat for 6–8 minutes to obtain a light, frothy mixture. Very gradually, add the clarified butter, whisking continuously. Season with salt and pepper.

» Pass the sauce through a strainer. Stir in the remaining tarragon.

SKILLET POTATO CAKE   RÖSTI

ONION RINGS   CAJUN SPICED POTATOES

CELERIAC RÉMOULADE
WIITH GRAPEFRUIT

RED CABBAGE SALAD WITH
WALNUTS

HOMEMADE FRIES

COLESLAW WITH GOLDEN RAISINS

All recipes serve 6.

SKILLET POTATO CAKE

14 oz (400 g) potatoes / 1 small carrot / ½ Granny Smith apple / 1 egg / 1 tbsp (15 g) heavy sour cream / 1½ tbsp (20 g) butter / 3 tbsp (45 ml) oil / salt, milled pepper

》 Peel and grate the potatoes, carrot, and apple. Arrange in a salad bowl. Add the egg, sour cream, salt, and pepper, and mix.

》 Heat the butter and oil in a skillet. Spread out the potato mixture in the skillet, pressing it down firmly with a spatula, and cook over moderate heat for 8–10 minutes. Using a plate, carefully turn the potato cake over to brown on the other side for 8–10 minutes. Place the potato cake on a baking sheet lined with wax paper and continue cooking for 10 minutes in the oven, preheated to 355 °F (180 °C.)

ROSTI

14 oz (400 g) mealy potatoes / 1 large onion / 1 egg, beaten / 2 pinches of nutmeg / knob of butter for frying / 3 tbsp (45 ml) oil for frying / salt, milled pepper

》 Peel the potatoes, then grate them finely. Peel and grate the onion. Squeeze both hard in your hands, pressing with your fingers to extract the excess liquid.

》 In a bowl, mix the potatoes and onions with the egg, nutmeg, salt, and pepper.

》 Heat the butter and oil in a large skillet. Place tablespoonfuls of the mixture in the skillet, flattening them slightly. Cook over moderate heat for 6–8 minutes each side. Serve immediately.

CELERIAC RÉMOULADE WITH GRAPEFRUIT

1 grapefruit / generous 1 lb (500 g) celeriac / 3 tbsp (45 g) mayonnaise

》 Peel the grapefruit. Cut into sections and remove the pith with a grapefruit knife, then chop the pulp into small pieces. Save any juice, and stir it into the mayonnaise.

》 Peel and grate the celeriac. Combine with the grapefruit in a salad bowl. Stir in the mayonnaise. Chill in the refrigerator for 2 hours before serving.

RED CABBAGE SALAD WITH WALNUTS

Generous 1 lb (500 g) red cabbage / 6 tbsp (90 ml) walnut oil / 1 tbsp (15 ml) runny honey / 4 tbsp (60 ml) red wine vinegar / ²⁄₃ cup (80 g) chopped walnuts / salt, milled pepper

》 Finely grate the red cabbage. Make a dressing in a bowl with the walnut oil, honey, vinegar, salt, and pepper. Add the red cabbage and walnuts. Mix well. Chill in the refrigerator for 2 hours before serving.

ONION RINGS

2 large white or yellow onions / 1 egg / 9 tbsp (80 g) all-purpose flour / 7 tbsp (100 ml) milk / 1 tbsp (15 ml) vegetable oil / salt / oil for frying

» Peel the onions and cut into rings about ⅛ in (3 mm) thick.

» Separate the egg and whisk the white. In a bowl, mix together the egg yolk, flour, vegetable oil, and a little salt. Carefully fold in the whisked egg white.

» Dip the onion rings in the batter, then fry for 1–2 minutes in the oil, pre-heated to 355 °F (180 °C.) Drain on paper towels, and serve immediately.

HOMEMADE FRIES

1¼ lb (600 g) mealy potatoes / salt / oil for frying

» Peel the potatoes, cut them into fries, and rinse in cold water. Pat dry with a clean dish towel.

» Lower the fries into plenty of oil, pre-heated to 300 °F (150 °C,) and cook for 7–8 minutes. Drain, then leave to cool.

» Just before serving, brown the fries for 4–5 minutes in the oil, re-heated to 355–375 °F (180–190 °C.) Drain on paper towels. Sprinkle with salt, and serve immediately.

CAJUN SPICED POTATOES

1¼ lb (600 g) small, waxy potatoes / ⅓ cup (50 g) all-purpose flour / 9 tbsp (130 ml) olive oil / ½ cup (60 g) Cajun seasoning / salt

» Wash the potatoes, but do not peel them. Cut each lengthwise, into 8 pieces.

» Bring a large saucepan of water to a boil with the flour and 3 tablespoons of olive oil. Put the potatoes in the water and cook for 4–5 minutes. Drain.

» Arrange the potatoes in an ovenproof dish. Add the Cajun seasoning and remaining oil, and season with salt to taste. Mix well, to coat the potatoes. Bake for 15–20 minutes in the oven, pre-heated to 355 °F (180 °C.)

COLESLAW WITH GOLDEN RAISINS

1 large carrot / 1 small onion / 14 oz (400 g) white cabbage / 3 oz (80 g) golden raisins / ¼ cup (60 g) homemade mayonnaise / prepared mustard (to taste) / 1 tbsp (15 ml) wine vinegar

» Peel and grate the carrot and onion. Peel and coarsely chop the cabbage. Mix in a bowl. Add the mayonnaise, prepared mustard, vinegar, and golden raisins. Chill in the refrigerator for 2 hours before serving.

BEEF!

PREPARATION : **20 minutes**
COOKING TIME : **10 minutes**

INGREDIENTS

Makes 6

- 6 plain burger buns (see recipe on p. 13)
- ½ onion
- 1¾–2 lb (800–900 g) ground beef
- 3 tbsp (45 ml) vegetable oil
- 3 tbsp (45 g) mayonnaise (see recipe on p. 16)
- 3 tbsp (45 g) ketchup (see recipe on p. 16)
- 2 cups (150 g) iceberg lettuce, washed and shredded
- 12 slices Cheddar cheese
- salt, milled pepper

CLASSIC CHEESEBURGER

》 Peel and finely chop the onion.

》 Season the ground beef with salt and pepper. Shape into 6 burgers the same size as the buns.

》 Heat the oil in a skillet and fry the burgers over moderate heat for 3–5 minutes on each side.

》 Cut the buns in half. Spread mayonnaise on the base and ketchup on the top half of each. Arrange half the lettuce on the bottom halves of the buns. Place a slice of Cheddar on top, then a burger, and finally another slice of cheese. Top with the remaining lettuce and onion. Close the buns and serve immediately.

Serve these burgers with homemade fries (see recipe on p. 21.)

CLASSIC AMERICAN BURGER

PREPARATION : **30 minutes**
COOKING TIME : **15 minutes**

INGREDIENTS

Makes 6

- 6 plain burger buns, topped with sesame seeds (see recipe on p. 13)
- 3 medium tomatoes
- 2 red onions
- 2 sweet pickled gherkins
- 1¾–2 lb (800–900 g) ground beef
- generous 1 tbsp (9 g) Cajun seasoning
- 3 tbsp (45 ml) vegetable oil
- 3 tbsp (45 g) mayonnaise (see recipe on p. 16)
- 3 tbsp (45 g) ketchup (see recipe on p. 16)
- 2 cups (150 g) iceberg lettuce, washed and shredded
- 6 slices Cheddar cheese
- salt, milled pepper

Wash the tomatoes and cut into rounds. Peel the onion and slice into rings ⅛–¼ inch (3–4 mm) thick. Slice the gherkins thinly into rounds.

≫ In a bowl, mix the ground beef with the Cajun seasoning and a pinch of salt. Shape into 6 burgers the same size as the buns.

≫ Heat the oil in a skillet and fry the onions over moderate heat for 4–5 minutes. Season with salt and pepper. Transfer to a plate.

≫ Fry the burgers in the skillet for 3–5 minutes on each side.

≫ Cut the buns in half. Spread mayonnaise on the base and ketchup on the top half of each. Arrange the lettuce on the bases. Add the onions. Lay a burger on top, then a slice of Cheddar, some tomato, and finally some gherkins. Close the

BLUE CHEESE BURGERS

PREPARATION : **30 minutes**
COOKING TIME : **10 minutes**

INGREDIENTS
Makes 6
- 6 walnut rolls (see recipe on p.12)
- 4 medium tomatoes
- 11 oz (300 g) blue cheese (e.g. Danish Blue)
- 3 tbsp (45 g) mayonnaise (see recipe on p. 16)
- 1 tbsp (15 g) strong prepared mustard
- 1 tbsp (15 ml) soy sauce
- 2–2¼ lb (900 g–1 kg) high quality ground beef (e.g. Charolais)
- 3 tbsp (45 ml) vegetable oil
- 2 cups (150 g) butterhead lettuce, washed and shredded
- salt, milled pepper

> Preheat the broiler.

> Wash the tomatoes and cut them into rounds.

> Cut the cheese into 6 medium-thick slices.

> In a bowl, mix together the mayonnaise, mustard, and soy sauce.

> Cut the rolls in half and lightly toast them in the broiler. Take them out, but do not turn the broiler off.

> Shape the ground beef into 6 burgers to fit the buns. Season with salt and pepper. Heat the oil in a skillet and fry the burgers for 3–5 minutes on each side.

> Place the cooked burgers on a baking sheet lined with wax paper, with a slice of cheese on top of each. Put the baking sheet in the broiler, fairly low down, and leave the door open.

> Spread the mustard sauce on the cut surfaces of the buns. Distribute the lettuce and tomatoes over the base of each.

> Take the burgers out of the broiler and place them on top of the tomatoes. Close the buns and serve immediately.

Triple-decker cheese burgers

PREPARATION : **40 minutes**
COOKING TIME : **15 minutes**

INGREDIENTS

Makes 6
- 6 plain burger buns, topped with sesame seeds (see recipe on p. 13)
- 3 large tomatoes
- 3 sweet pickled gherkins
- 7 oz (200 g) Comté Gruyère
- 2¾ lb (1.2 kg) ground beef
- 3 tbsp (45 ml) sunflower oil
- 12 slices Canadian / smoked back bacon
- 6 tbsp (90 g) mayonnaise (see recipe on p. 16)
- few drops Tabasco® sauce
- small bunch fresh herbs, finely chopped
- 3 tbsp (45 g) ketchup (see recipe on p. 16)
- 2 cups (150 g) butterhead or iceberg lettuce, washed and shredded
- salt, milled pepper

≫ Preheat the broiler.

≫ Wash the tomatoes and cut them into slices. Cut the gherkins into rounds. Cut the cheese into 18 thin slices.

≫ Season the meat with salt and pepper. Shape 18 very thin burgers, the same size as the buns.

≫ Heat the oil in a skillet and fry the burgers for 2–3 minutes on each side. Keep hot.

≫ Place the bacon slices on a baking sheet lined with wax paper and cook for 3–4 minutes in the broiler. Keep hot in the broiler, with the door open.

≫ In a bowl, mix together the herby mayonnaise, Tabasco®, and chopped herbs.

≫ Cut the buns in half. Spread ketchup on the base and mayonnaise on the top half of each.

≫ Arrange half the lettuce on the base of the buns. Place a burger on top, then some tomatoes, gherkin rounds, and a slice of cheese. Add another burger, slice of cheese, and 2 slices of bacon. Finish with a burger, another slice of cheese, and the remaining lettuce. Close the buns and serve immediately.

For the real gourmands: spread a little homemade mayonnaise and ketchup on each burger!

PREPARATION : **40 minutes**
COOKING TIME : **20 minutes**

TEX-MEX BURGERS

INGREDIENTS

Makes 6

- 6 burger buns: paprika or plain
  (see recipes on p. 13)
- 2 onions
- 2 red bell peppers
- 1 yellow bell pepper
- 2 cloves garlic
- 3 tbsp (45 ml) olive oil
- salt
- 1 tbsp (8 g) paprika
- 1¾–2 lb (800–900 g) ground beef
- milled pepper
- 3 tbsp (45 ml) vegetable oil
- 3 tbsp (45 g) chili sauce (see
  recipe on p. 17)
- 6 slices Cheddar cheese

》 Peel the onions, seed the bell peppers, and thinly slice. Peel and mince the garlic.

》 Heat the olive oil in a skillet and fry the bell peppers, onions, and garlic over moderate heat for 10 minutes, stirring from time to time. Season with salt and add half the paprika. Cover with aluminum foil and keep hot in the skillet.

》 Preheat the broiler.

》 In a bowl, mix together the ground beef, the remaining paprika, salt, and pepper. Shape the mixture into 6 burgers, to fit the buns.

》 Heat the vegetable oil in a skillet and fry the burgers for 3–5 minutes on each side.

》 Cut the buns in half, then lightly toast them in the broiler.

》 Spread chili sauce over the cut surfaces of the buns. Distribute half the onion, bell pepper, and garlic mixture over the base of each. Add a burger, a slice of Cheddar, and then the remaining bell pepper mixture. Close the buns and serve immediately.

Burgers with ham and cheese

PREPARATION : **30 minutes**
COOKING TIME : **15 minutes**

INGREDIENTS

Makes 6

- 6 burger buns: curry, paprika, or plain (see recipes on p. 13)
- 2 beefsteak tomatoes
- 5½ oz (150 g) Ossau-Iraty (semi-hard ewe milk cheese)
- 1¼–2 lb (800–900 g) ground beef
- 2 tbsp (15 g) mild chili powder
- salt
- 3 tbsp (45 ml) vegetable oil
- 6 slices air-dried smoked ham (e.g. Bayonne ham)
- 3 tbsp (45 g) mayonnaise (see recipe on p. 16)
- 2 cups (150 g) butterhead or iceberg lettuce, washed and shredded

》 Wash the tomatoes and cut them into rounds. Cut the cheese into thin slices.

》 Preheat the broiler.

》 In a bowl, mix together the ground beef, 1 tablespoon of chili powder, and a pinch of salt. Shape the mixture into 6 burgers, to fit the buns.

》 Heat the oil in a skillet and fry the burgers for 3–5 minutes on each side.

》 Lay the ham slices on a baking sheet lined with wax paper. Brown them lightly in the broiler for 3–4 minutes. Remove the baking sheet, but do not turn the broiler off.

》 Cut the buns in half, then lightly toast them in the broiler.

》 In a bowl, mix the remaining chili powder with the mayonnaise.

》 Spread the chili-flavored mayonnaise on both cut surfaces of the buns. Distribute the lettuce and the tomato rounds over the base of each. Place a burger on top, followed by a slice each of ham and cheese. Close the buns and serve immediately.

CONTINENTAL BURGERS

PREPARATION : **30 minutes**
COOKING TIME : **15 minutes**

INGREDIENTS

Makes 6

- 6 mixed-seed rolls (available from your baker)
- 12 slices Canadian /smoked back bacon
- 2—2¼ lb (900 g—1 kg) ground beef
- 3 tbsp (45 ml) vegetable oil
- 6 eggs
- 1½ tbsp (25 g) butter
- 3 tbsp (45 g) mayonnaise (see recipe on p. 16)
- 3 tbsp (45 g) ketchup (see recipe on p. 16)
- 2 cups (150 g) butterhead or iceberg lettuce, washed and shredded
- 6 slices Cheddar cheese
- salt, milled pepper

》 Preheat the broiler.

》 Lay the bacon slices on a baking sheet lined with wax paper Brown them in the broiler for 3 minutes. Remove the baking sheet, but leave the broiler on.

》 Cut the rolls in half and lightly toast them in the broiler.

》 Shape the ground beef into 6 burgers to fit the rolls. Season with salt and pepper. Heat the vegetable oil in a skillet and fry the burgers for 3—5 minutes on each side.

》 Meanwhile, in another skillet, fry the eggs in the butter. Season with salt and pepper.

》 Spread mayonnaise on the base and ketchup on the top half of each roll. Distribute the lettuce over the base of each. Place a burger on top, followed by a slice of Cheddar, a fried egg, and 2 slices of bacon. Close the rolls and serve immediately.

Mini burgers

PREPARATION : **30 minutes**
COOKING TIME : **10 minutes**

INGREDIENTS

Makes 12

- 12 small rolls, weighing about 2 oz (50 g) each: plain, or topped with sesame or poppy seeds (see recipes on p. 12)
- generous 1 lb (500 g) ground beef
- 5½ oz (150 g) Mimolette, Colby or Cheshire cheese
- 3 tbsp (45 ml) vegetable oil
- 3 tbsp (45 g) mayonnaise (see recipe on p. 16)
- 3 tbsp (45 g) ketchup (see recipe on p. 16)
- 1½ cups (120 g) butterhead lettuce, washed and shredded
- salt, milled pepper

≫ Season the ground beef with salt and pepper, then shape into 12 mini burgers to fit the rolls.

≫ Using a vegetable peeler, shave off thin slivers of cheese.

≫ Preheat the broiler.

≫ Heat the oil in a skillet and fry the burgers over moderate heat for 5–7 minutes. Keep hot.

≫ Cut the rolls in half and lightly toast them in the broiler.

≫ Spread mayonnaise on the base and ketchup on the top half of each roll. Arrange the lettuce on the bases. Add a mini burger and a few shavings of cheese to each. Close the rolls and serve immediately.

ASIAN-STYLE BURGERS

PREPARATION : **40 minutes**
COOKING TIME : **20 minutes**

INGREDIENTS

Makes 6

- 6 rolls: paprika or plain (see recipes on p. 13)
- 2 red bell peppers
- 1 eggplant
- 7 tbsp (100 ml) olive oil
- 1 small red onion
- 1¼–2 lb (800–900 g) ground beef
- 1 tsp (2.5 g) ground cumin
- 1 tbsp (8 g) cumin seeds
- 3 tbsp (45 ml) vegetable oil
- 1 bunch cilantro
- 1 bunch flatleaf parsley
- 3 tbsp (45 g) mayonnaise (see recipe on p. 16)
- 1 tbsp (15 g) harissa paste
- 6 slices Cheddar cheese
- salt, milled pepper

≫ Seed and thinly slice the bell peppers. Wash the eggplant and slice into rounds ⅛–¼ in (4–5 mm) thick.

≫ Heat 4 tablespoons of olive oil in a skillet and brown the eggplant slices over moderate heat for 4–5 minutes. Drain on paper towels, then cover with a sheet of aluminum foil and keep hot.

≫ Heat the remaining olive oil in the same skillet and cook the bell peppers over moderate heat for 6–8 minutes. Keep hot, together with the eggplant slices.

≫ Preheat the broiler.

≫ Peel and finely chop the onion.

≫ In a bowl, mix together the ground beef, onion, ground cumin, cumin seeds, salt, and pepper. Shape into 6 burgers, to fit the buns.

≫ Heat the vegetable oil in the skillet and fry the burgers for 3–5 minutes on each side.

≫ Meanwhile, wash, chop and mix together the herbs. Combine the mayonnaise and harissa in a bowl.

≫ Cut the buns in half and lightly toast them in the broiler.

≫ Spread the harissa-flavored mayonnaise on the cut surfaces of the buns. Cover the lower halves of the buns with eggplant slices. Place a burger on top, then add the bell peppers, a slice of Cheddar, and the cilantro-parsley mixture. Close the buns and serve immediately.

PREPARATION : **40 minutes**
COOKING TIME : **20 minutes**

THAI-STYLE BEEF BURGERS

INGREDIENTS

Makes 6

- 6 sesame rolls (see recipe on p. 12)
- 11 oz (300 g) shiitake mushrooms
- ⅓ cup (75 ml) vegetable oil
- 1 tbsp (15 ml) runny honey
- 1¾ lb (800 g) ground beef
- 1 tbsp (8 g) grated fresh ginger
- 2 tbsp (30 ml) oyster sauce
- ⅔ cup (150 ml) sweet soy sauce
- 3 tbsp (45 g) mayonnaise (see recipe on p. 16)
- 1 tsp (5 g) wasabi
- 1½ cups (120 g) butterhead lettuce, washed and shredded
- 6 slices Cheddar cheese
- salt, milled pepper

≫ Dry and thinly slice the mushrooms. Heat half the oil in a skillet and fry over moderate heat for 3 minutes. Add the honey, then season with salt and pepper. Mix well and continue cooking until lightly caramelized. Keep hot.

≫ In a bowl, mix the ground beef, ginger, oyster sauce, pepper, and a little salt. Shape into 6 burgers, to fit the rolls.

≫ Preheat the broiler.

≫ Heat the remaining oil in a skillet and fry the burgers for 2–3 minutes on each side. Remove the fat from the skillet and pour the soy sauce over the burgers. Cook over gentle heat for 4 minutes, spooning the sauce over the burgers to coat them slightly. Keep hot.

≫ In a bowl, combine the mayonnaise and wasabi.

≫ Cut the rolls in half, then lightly toast them in the broiler.

≫ Spead the wasabi-flavored mayonnaise over both cut surfaces of the rolls. Distribute the lettuce over the base of each. Place a burger on top, then add a slice of cheese and the hot mushrooms. Close the rolls and serve immediately.

Carpaccio burgers with broiled vegetables

INGREDIENTS

Makes 6

- 6 plain rolls, topped with caraway or cumin seeds (see recipes on p. 13)
- 2 zucchini
- 1 large eggplant
- 7 tbsp (100 ml) olive oil
- generous 1–1¼ lb (500–600 g) raw beef for carpaccio, very thinly sliced
- juice of 1 lemon
- ¼ cup (60 g) mayonnaise (see recipe on p. 16)
- 2 tbsp (30 g) prepared mustard (your choice)
- 3½ oz (100 g) Parmesan
- 1½ cups (120 g) arugula
- salt, milled pepper

》 Wash the zucchini and eggplant, then slice into rounds $^1/_{16}$–$^1/_8$ in (2–3 mm) thick. Combine in a bowl with half the olive oil, salt, and pepper.

》 Brown the zucchini and eggplant rounds in a broiler or skillet, without oil, for about 5 minutes on each side. They should remain crisp.

》 Arrange the carpaccio slices on a plate.

》 In a bowl, mix the remaining oil, lemon juice, salt, and pepper. Brush this marinade over the meat, and chill in the refrigerator for 10 minutes.

》 Combine the mayonnaise and mustard.

》 Use a vegetable peeler to make shavings of Parmesan.

》 Cut the rolls in half. Spread the mustard-flavored mayonnaise on the base of each. Add the broiled vegetables, followed by the marinated carpaccio slices, and then some arugula. Sprinkle with Parmesan shavings. Close the rolls and serve immediately.

MOUNTAIN BURGERS

INGREDIENTS

Makes 6

- 6 rolls : Gruyère or bacon flavor
  (see recipes on p. 12)
- 6½ oz (180 g) Râclette
  (Emmental-style cheese)
- 7 tbsp (100 ml) light cream
- 2 sweet pickled gherkins
- 1¾–2 lb (800–900 g) ground beef
- 3 tbsp (45 ml) vegetable oil
- 2 cups (150 g) Batavian endive /
  escarole, washed and shredded
- salt, milled pepper

≫ Remove the rind from the Râclette. Bring the cream to a boil in a large saucepan. Add 1–1½ oz (30–40 g) of the cheese and cook gently for 4–5 minutes, stirring constantly, until it melts. Pour the sauce into a bowl and place in the refrigerator for 30 minutes, to thicken slightly.

≫ Cut the remaining cheese into 6 fairly thick slices. Slice the gherkins into thin rounds.

≫ Preheat the broiler.

≫ Season the ground beef with salt and pepper. Shape into 6 burgers, to fit the rolls.

≫ Heat the oil in a skillet and fry the burgers over moderate heat for 3–5 minutes on each side. Cover the skillet with a sheet of aluminum foil and keep hot.

≫ Cut the rolls in half and lightly toast them in the broiler.

≫ Spread the cheese sauce over the cut surfaces of the rolls. Distribute the endive and gherkins over the base of each. Place a burger on top, followed by a slice of cheese. Close the rolls and serve immediately.

CHICKEN, LAMB, ETC!

CRUNCHY CHICKEN BURGERS

PREPARATION : **45 minutes**
COOKING TIME : **10 minutes**

INGREDIENTS

Makes 6

- 6 olive or mixed-seed rolls (see recipe on p. 12)
- 2 eggs
- 4 oz (120 g) cornflakes
- 7 tbsp (60 g) all-purpose flour
- 6 chicken breasts, 4 oz (120 g) each
- oil for frying
- 3 medium tomatoes
- 5½ oz (150 g) caraway- or cumin-flavor Gouda
- 6 tbsp (90 g) chili sauce (see recipe on p. 17)
- 1½ cups (120 g) Batavian endive or butterhead lettuce, washed and shredded
- salt, milled pepper

≫ Take three shallow bowls; beat the eggs in one, crush the cornflakes and place them in another, and spread the seasoned flour evenly in the third.

≫ Flatten the chicken breasts slightly. Coat them first in the flour, then in the beaten egg, and finally in the cornflakes.

≫ Heat the oil in a deep-fat fryer.

≫ Wash the tomatoes and cut them into rounds. Cut the cheese into 6 thin slices.

≫ Deep-fry the chicken breasts in very hot oil for 4–5 minutes. Drain on paper towels.

≫ Cut the rolls in half. Spread chili sauce over the cut surfaces. Distribute half the salad greens and tomatoes over the bases. Place a fried chicken breast on top, then a slice of cheese. Finish with the remaining salad greens. Close the rolls and serve immediately.

Serve these burgers with Cajun spiced potatoes (see recipe on p. 21.)

CHICKEN BURGERS WITH GOAT CHEESE

PREPARATION : **40 minutes**
+ 30 minutes' refrigeration
COOKING TIME : **15 minutes**

INGREDIENTS

Makes 6
- 6 curry and sesame buns (see recipe on p. 13)
- 1 tbsp (15 g) heavy sour cream
- 7 small, ripe goat cheeses
- 5 tbsp (75 ml) olive oil
- 1 tsp (2.5 g) mild chili powder
- 2 pinches curry powder
- 6 chicken breasts, 4 oz (120 g) each
- 1 small, raw beet
- 2 carrots
- generous 1 cup (100 g) butterhead lettuce, washed and shredded
- salt, milled pepper

≫ Bring the sour cream to a boil in a small saucepan. Add one of the goat cheeses and bring to a boil once more, stirring constantly for 2 minutes until the cheese melts. Season with salt and pepper. Pour the sauce into a bowl and chill in the refrigerator for 30 minutes, so that it thickens slightly.

≫ Combine 3 tablespoons of olive oil with the chili powder, curry powder, and a pinch of salt on a dinner plate. Flatten the chicken breasts slightly, place them on the plate, then coat them thoroughly on each side with the spiced oil.

≫ Preheat the broiler.

≫ Peel the beet and the carrots, then cut them into fine strips. Mix in a bowl with the remaining oil, salt, and pepper.

≫ Heat a skillet and brown the chicken breasts that have been coated with the spiced oil over medium heat for 6–7 minutes on each side.

≫ Cut the buns in half and lightly toast them in the broiler.

≫ Spread the goat cheese sauce over the cut surfaces of the buns. Distribute the lettuce over the base of each. Place a chicken breast on top, followed by a goat cheese, and a little of the beet-carrot mixture. Close the buns and serve immediately.

Spicy lamb burgers

INGREDIENTS

Makes 6

- 6 plain or curry sesame buns
  (see recipes on p. 13)
- 1 large eggplant
- ½ onion
- 2 cloves garlic
- 4 oz (120 g) Cheddar cheese
- 1¾–2 lb (800–900 g) ground lamb
- 7 tbsp (100 ml) olive oil
- 1 tbsp (8 g) curry powder
- ¼ cup (60 g) mayonnaise
  (see recipe on p. 16)
- generous 1 cup (100 g)
  butterhead lettuce, washed and
  shredded
- salt, milled pepper

≫ Wash the eggplant and cut into rounds $\frac{1}{16}$ inch (2 mm) thick. Peel the onion and garlic, and chop finely. Cut the cheese into slivers.

≫ In a bowl, mix together the ground lamb, onion, garlic, salt, and pepper. Shape into 6 burgers, to fit the rolls.

≫ Put half the olive oil into a skillet and cook the eggplant rounds for 4–5 minutes on each side. Season with salt and pepper. Transfer to a plate.

≫ Heat the remaining olive oil in the skillet and fry the burgers for 6–8 minutes on each side. Towards the end of the cooking time, sprinkle with half the curry powder.

≫ Preheat the broiler.

≫ In a bowl, combine the remaining curry powder with the mayonnaise.

≫ Cut the buns in half and lightly toast them in the broiler.

≫ Spread the curry mayonnaise over the cut surfaces of the buns. Distribute the lettuce over the base of each and add a few eggplant rounds. Place a burger on top, followed by cheese slivers. Close the buns and serve immediately.

CHICKEN AND CASHEW BURGERS

PREPARATION : **30 minutes**
CHILLING : **2 hours**
COOKING TIME : **20 minutes**

INGREDIENTS

Makes 6

- 6 plain sesame buns
  (see recipe on p. 13)
- 7 tbsp (100 ml) olive oil
- 2 tbsp (30 g) red curry paste
- salt
- 6 chicken breasts, 4 oz (120 g)
  each
- 2 red onions
- 1¾ oz (50 g) cashews
- 1 large, sweet, pickled gherkin
- 3 tbsp (45 g) mayonnaise
  (see recipe on p. 16)
- 2 cups (150 g) butterhead or
  iceberg lettuce, washed and
  shredded
- 6 slices Cheddar cheese

≫ In a dish, mix half the olive oil with 1½ tablespoons of curry paste and a pinch of salt to make a marinade. Place the chicken breasts in the marinade and coat them well on both sides. Cover the dish with plastic wrap and chill in the refrigerator for 2 hours.

≫ Peel and finely chop the onions. Heat the remaining oil in a skillet and fry the onions over medium heat for 4–5 minutes. Season with salt. Transfer to a plate.

≫ Transfer the chicken breasts and marinade to a skillet and cook over medium heat for 10–15 minutes, turning frequently. Coarsely chop the cashews and mix with the cooked chicken breasts in the skillet.

≫ Preheat the broiler.

≫ Cut the buns in half and lightly toast them in the broiler.

≫ Cut the gherkin into thin rounds.

≫ In a bowl, combine the remaining curry paste with the mayonnaise.

≫ Spread the curry mayonnaise over the cut surfaces of the buns. Distribute the lettuce and onions over the base of each. Place a chicken breast on top with some of the cashews, a slice of cheese, and a few gherkin rounds. Close the buns and serve immediately.

PREPARATION : **40 minutes**
COOKING TIME : **20 minutes**

SWEET-AND-SOUR PORK BURGERS

INGREDIENTS

Makes 6

- 6 plain rolls (see recipe on p. 12)
- 3 oz (80 g) salted peanuts, roasted skin on
- 1 large red onion
- 7 tbsp (100 ml) olive oil
- 2 tbsp (30 ml) runny honey
- 2 tbsp (30 ml) wine vinegar
- 1½–1¾ lb (700–800 g) ground pork or sausagemeat
- 5½ oz (150 g) cumin-flavor Gouda
- 6 tbsp (90 ml) prepared sweet-and-sour sauce
- 1½ cups (120 g) butterhead lettuce, washed and shredded
- salt, milled pepper

≫ Coarsely chop the peanuts. Peel and finely chop the onion.

≫ Heat 3 tablespoons of olive oil in a skillet and sweat the onion for 5 minutes, until transparent. Add the peanuts, honey, salt, and pepper. Mix well and cook over medium heat for 3 minutes, until lightly caramelized. Stir the vinegar into the skillet and reduce over high heat for 2 minutes. Turn off the heat and allow to cool.

≫ Pour the mixture into a bowl, add the ground pork, and combine. Season with salt and pepper. Shape into 6 burgers, to fit the rolls.

≫ Heat the remaining olive oil in a skillet and fry the burgers over medium heat for 8–10 minutes, turning frequently.

≫ Preheat the broiler.

≫ Cut the Gouda into thin slices.

≫ Cut the rolls in half and lightly toast them in the broiler.

≫ Spread the sweet-and-sour sauce over the cut surfaces of the rolls. Distribute the lettuce over the base of each. Place a burger on top, then some Gouda slices. Close the rolls and serve immediately.

BREAKFAST BURGERS

PREPARATION : **40 minutes**
COOKING TIME : **20 minutes**

INGREDIENTS

Makes 6

- 6 plain rolls (see recipe on p. 12)
- 6 eggs
- 3 tbsp (45 ml) vegetable oil
- 1½ tbsp (20–25 g) butter
- 6 chipolatas
- 6 large slices bacon
- 4 tbsp (60 g) ketchup (see recipe on p. 16)
- 1½ cups (120 g) butterhead or romaine lettuce, washed and shredded
- 6 tbsp (90 g) mayonnaise (see recipe on p. 16)
- 6 slices Cheddar cheese
- salt, milled pepper

≫ In a bowl, beat the eggs with salt and pepper. Heat half the oil and the butter in a skillet, pour the beaten eggs over, and cook over medium heat for 5–7 minutes, stirring occasionally with a fork, until the omelet is lightly done. Leave in the skillet and keep hot.

≫ Heat the remaining oil in another skillet and fry the chipolatas for 8–10 minutes. Transfer to a plate and keep hot.

≫ Drain the fat from the skillet and dry-fry the bacon slices for 2 minutes either side.

≫ Preheat the broiler. Cut the rolls in half and toast them lightly in the broiler.

≫ Spread ketchup on the base of each roll, then add some lettuce. Spread mayonnaise on the top half of each roll. Cut the omelet into 6 pieces. Add a piece of omelet, a slice of bacon, a chipolata (cut in half), and a slice of cheese. Close the rolls and serve immediately.

Serve these burgers with a side of red cabbage salad with walnuts (see recipe on p. 20.)

BURGOS
cordero y
León), pimiento
de cabra, tomate,
8,80€
Burger de 200g
pepinillos,
cogollos,
y cebolla 8,90€

CHICKEN CAESAR BURGERS

PREPARATION : **30 minutes**
COOKING TIME : **25 minutes**

INGREDIENTS

Makes 6

- 6 poppy seed rolls (see recipe on p. 12)
- 2 cloves garlic
- 5½ oz (150 g) Parmesan
- 2 whole eggs + 1 egg yolk
- ⅔ cup (150 ml) olive oil
- 6 small chicken breasts
- 1 oz (30 g) capers
- 1 tbsp (15 ml) Worcestershire sauce
- 1½ tbsp (20–25 g) strong prepared mustard
- juice of ½ lemon
- scant 3 cups (200 g) romaine lettuce, washed and coarsely shredded
- salt, milled pepper

≫ Peel and finely chop the garlic. Cut the Parmesan into shavings with a vegetable peeler.

≫ Hard-cook the whole eggs for 10 minutes in a pan of boiling, salted water. Cool them under cold running water before peeling.

≫ Heat 3 tablespoons of olive oil in a skillet and fry the chicken breasts over medium heat for 12–14 minutes, turning frequently. Season with salt and pepper. Cut them lengthwise into strips.

≫ Preheat the broiler.

≫ Chop the hard-cooked eggs and place in a deep bowl. Add the egg yolk, capers, Worcestershire sauce, mustard, lemon juice, garlic, the remaining oil, salt, and pepper. Pulse in a blender to make a Caesar dressing (add a little cold water if it becomes too thick.)

≫ Cut the rolls in half and toast them lightly in the broiler.

≫ Spread some of the Caesar dressing over the base of each roll. Add some lettuce, then the chicken strips. Top with more Caesar dressing and Parmesan shavings. Close the rolls and serve immediately.

PREPARATION : **30 minutes**
COOKING TIME : **20 minutes**

Italian burgers

INGREDIENTS

Makes 6
- 6 ciabatta rolls (available from your baker)
- generous 1 cup (100 g) arugula
- 3 plum tomatoes
- 2 cloves garlic
- 15 basil leaves
- 5½ oz (150 g) pecorino
- ¼ cup (60 g) mayonnaise (see recipe on p. 16)
- 12 thin slices pancetta
- 2 lb (900 g) ground veal shoulder
- 3 tbsp (45 ml) olive oil
- salt, milled pepper

≫ Wash the arugula. Wash the tomatoes and cut them into rounds. Peel and finely chop the garlic. Wash and chop the basil. Use a vegetable peeler to cut the pecorino into shavings.

≫ In a bowl, mix together the mayonnaise, garlic, and basil.

≫ Preheat the broiler.

≫ Dry-fry the pancetta in a skillet over medium heat for 2 minutes. Transfer to a plate and set aside.

≫ Season the ground veal with salt and pepper. Shape into 6 burgers, to fit the rolls.

≫ Cut the rolls in half and lightly toast them in the broiler.

≫ Heat the olive oil in a skillet and fry the burgers for 6–8 minutes on each side. Keep hot.

≫ Spread the basil mayonnaise over the cut surfaces of the rolls. Distribute the arugula over the base of each. Place a veal burger on top, followed by a few tomato rounds and 2 slices of pancetta. Sprinkle with pecorino shavings. Close the rolls and serve immediately.

HERBY VEAL BURGERS

PREPARATION : **40 minutes**
COOKING TIME : **25 minutes**

INGREDIENTS

Makes 6

- 6 olive or curry rolls (see recipes
  on p. 12)
- 6 cloves garlic
- 7 tbsp (100 ml) light cream
- 2 lb (900 g) whole short
  tenderloin of veal
- 3 tbsp (45 ml) olive oil
- 1 shallot
- few mint leaves
- 1 sprig parsley
- 1 tbsp (15 g) mayonnaise
  (see recipe on p. 16)
- 1 pot Greek yogurt
- 3 pinches chili powder
- 3 tomatoes
- 2 cups (150 g) butterhead or
  iceberg lettuce, washed and
  shredded
- 6 slices Cheddar cheese
- salt, milled pepper

≫ Peel 5 of the garlic cloves and cut them in half, removing the bitter green sprouts. Place them in a saucepan and cover with cold water. Bring to a boil, drain in a colander, and refresh under cold running water. Repeat the process 4 times.

≫ Pour the cream into a saucepan. Add the prepared, softened garlic, salt, and pepper. Cook over gentle heat for 6–8 minutes. Stir constantly, to obtain a thick garlic cream. Leave to cool.

≫ Season the veal tenderloin with salt and pepper. Heat the olive oil in a skillet and brown the meat for 3 minutes on each side; then cook over medium heat for 10–12 minutes, turning frequently. Wrap in aluminum foil and leave to rest for 15 minutes. Then cut the tenderloin into very thin slices and keep hot.

≫ Peel and finely chop the remaining garlic clove, together with the shallot. Chop the mint and parsley. In a bowl, mix together the mayonnaise, yogurt, garlic, shallot, mint, parsley, chili powder, salt, and pepper.

≫ Preheat the broiler. Cut the rolls in half and lightly toast them in the broiler.

≫ Wash the tomatoes and cut them into rounds.

≫ Spread the garlic cream over the base of each roll. Distribute the lettuce on top, then add a few tomato rounds. Place some of the veal slices and a slice of cheese on top of the lettuce. Add a little of the chili mayonnaise. Cover the rolls and serve immediately.

DUCK CONFIT BURGERS

PREPARATION : 20 minutes
COOKING TIME : 40 minutes

INGREDIENTS

Makes 6

- 6 plain rolls (see recipe on p. 12)
- 4 preserved duck legs, with fat (i.e. duck confit, available in pots from good supermarkets)
- 1¼ lb (600 g) red potatoes
- 2 tbsp (30 g) mayonnaise (see recipe on p. 16)
- 1 tbsp (15 g) sweet prepared mustard
- 8 walnuts
- generous 1 cup (100 g) butterhead lettuce, washed and shredded
- salt, milled pepper

≫ Preheat the oven to 320 °F (160 °C).

≫ Arrange the whole duck legs with a little of their fat in an ovenproof dish. Put the dish in the oven and heat through for 20 minutes.

≫ Peel the potatoes, slice them thinly into rounds, and rinse in a colander under hot running water (from the kettle). Sauté in a skillet with 2 tablespoons of duck fat, for 20 minutes. Season with salt and pepper.

≫ In a bowl, combine the mayonnaise with the mustard.

≫ Take the duck legs out of the oven. Preheat the broiler.

≫ Chop the walnuts. Remove the skin from the duck legs, then shred the meat. Mix this with the walnuts. Keep hot, with a little duck fat in the ovenproof dish.

≫ Cut the rolls in half and lightly toast them in the broiler.

≫ Spread some mustard mayonnaise over the base of each roll. Then add some potato rounds, duck meat, and lettuce. Close the rolls and serve immediately.

INGREDIENTS

Makes 6

- 6 plain rolls with mixed-seeds topping (see recipe on p. 12)
- 2 large duck breasts
- 1 large bunch fresh mixed herbs (chervil, tarragon, chives...)
- 2 tbsp (30 ml) prepared French dressing (vinaigrette)
- 6½ oz (180 g) ready-made duck foie gras (canned or potted)
- 7 oz (200 g) pot of caramelized onions or onion marmalade
- 3 tbsp (45 g) barbecue sauce
- salt, milled pepper

DUCK CHIC BURGERS

》 Remove any fat from the duck breasts, then score the skin in a crisscross pattern with the tip of a sharp knife. Season with salt and pepper.

》 Arrange the duck breasts, skin-side down, in a very hot skillet, with no added fat. Cook for 6–8 minutes, then turn them over and cook for a further 5 minutes. Wrap each in a sheet of aluminum foil and allow to rest for 10 minutes.

》 Preheat the broiler.

》 Coarsely chop the herbs and mix them with the vinaigrette in a bowl.

》 Cut the foie gras into very thin slices and the duck breasts lengthwise into thin strips.

》 Cut the rolls in half and lightly toast them in the broiler.

》 Distribute the caramelized onions or onion marmalade over the base of each roll. Place strips of duck on top, then some slices of foie gras. Top with the herb mixture. Spread barbecue sauce over the top half of each roll. Close the rolls and serve immediately.

TANDOORI BURGERS

PREPARATION : 30 minutes
MARINADE : 24 hours
COOKING TIME : 40—45 minutes

INGREDIENTS

Makes 6

For the marinade
- 1 pot plain yogurt
- 1 tbsp (8 g) tandoori spice
- 1 clove garlic, minced
- juice of 1 lemon
- salt, milled pepper

For the burgers
- 6 olive rolls (see recipe on p. 12)
- 6 chicken escalopes, 4—5 oz
  (120—140 g) each
- 2 red onions
- 3 tbsp (45 ml) olive oil
- 1 tbsp (15 ml) runny honey
- 6 tbsp (90 g) mayonnaise
  (see recipe on p. 16)
- 1 tsp (2.5 g) tandoori masala
  (powdered spice)
- juice of 1 lemon
- 2 sweet, pickled gherkins
- 1⅔ cups (120 g) butterhead or
  romaine lettuce, washed and
  shredded
- 5½ oz (150 g) Cheddar cheese

》 Prepare the marinade 24 hours in advance: in a bowl, mix the yogurt, tandoori spice, garlic, lemon juice, salt, and pepper. Place the chicken escalopes in a deep bowl. Add the marinade, coating the meat well. Cover with plastic wrap and chill in the refrigerator overnight.

》 Shortly before you start cooking, preheat the oven to 320 °F (160 °C).

》 Drain the escalopes from the marinade and lay them on a baking sheet lined with wax paper. Cook in the oven for 40—45 minutes.

》 Meanwhile, peel and finely chop the onions. Heat the olive oil in a skillet and cook the onions over low heat for 15—20 minutes, until browned and transparent. Add the honey at the end of the cooking time and allow the onions to caramelize lightly. Keep hot.

》 In a bowl, combine the mayonnaise, tandoori spice, and lemon juice.

》 Cut the gherkins into rounds.

》 Cut the rolls in half. Spread the tandoori mayonnaise over their cut surfaces. Distribute the lettuce and onions over the base of each roll. Place a chicken escalope, cut into several pieces, on top, followed by the cheese, then a few gherkin rounds. Close the rolls and serve immediately.

PICCATA BURGERS

PREPARATION : **30 minutes**
COOKING TIME : **12 minutes**

INGREDIENTS

Makes 6

- 6 sun-dried tomato or plain buns
  (see recipes on p. 13)
- 1 eggplant
- ⅓ cup (75 ml) olive oil
- 3 tbsp (45 g) mayonnaise
  (see recipe on p. 16)
- juice of 1 lemon
- 6 very thin veal escalopes
- 4 oz (120g) piece pecorino
  (ewe cheese)
- 12 quarters sun-dried tomatoes
  in oil
- generous 1 cup (100 g) small,
  young salad greens, washed
- salt, milled pepper

≫ Preheat the broiler.

≫ Wash the eggplant and slice thinly. Heat half the olive oil in a skillet and cook the eggplant over medium heat for 3–4 minutes on each side. Season with salt and pepper.

≫ Cut the buns in half and toast them lightly in the broiler.

≫ In a bowl, mix the mayonnaise, half the lemon juice, salt, and pepper.

≫ Cut the veal escalopes into large pieces. Season with salt and pepper. Heat the remaining olive oil in a skillet and fry the veal pieces over medium heat for 2 minutes on each side. Remove from the heat, then sprinkle with the remaining lemon juice. Cover the skillet with aluminum foil and keep hot.

≫ Use a vegetable peeler to cut the pecorino into shavings. Drain the tomato quarters and dice them.

≫ Spread the lemon mayonnaise liberally over the cut surfaces of the buns. Distribute the salad greens over the base of each, followed by some eggplant slices, veal pieces, and diced tomatoes. Sprinkle with pecorino shavings. Close the buns and serve immediately.

KOFTE BURGERS

PREPARATION : **30 minutes**
COOKING TIME : **15 minutes**

INGREDIENTS

Makes 6
- 6 curry or plain buns (see recipes on p. 13)
- 1 onion
- 1¾ lb (800 g) ground lamb
- ½ bunch cilantro
- 2 tbsp (15 g) cumin seeds
- 3 tbsp (45 ml) olive oil
- 2 tomatoes
- 6 oz (180 g) Cheddar cheese
- 6 tbsp (90 g) white sauce with herbs (see recipe on p. 16)
- 2 cups (150 g) butterhead lettuce, washed and shredded
- salt, milled pepper

≫ Peel and finely chop the onion. Coarsely chop or shred the cilantro.

≫ Mix the ground lamb in a bowl with the onion, cilantro, cumin seeds, salt, and pepper.

≫ Shape by hand into 18 small patties; heat the olive oil in a skillet and fry them over medium heat for 3–4 minutes on each side. Keep hot.

≫ Preheat the broiler.

≫ Wash the tomatoes and cut them into small cubes. Cut the cheese into 6 thin slices.

≫ Cut the buns in half and toast them lightly in the broiler.

≫ Spread the herb sauce over the cut surfaces of the buns. Distribute the lettuce and the tomato cubes over the base of each; place 3 meat patties on top, and finish with a slice of cheese. Close the buns and serve immediately.

These burgers go well with rösti or onion rings (see recipes on pp. 20–21).

MEZCLA ESPECIAL
CHIP MIX
El SALMÓN ES
DEL MERCADO DE
CATERINA
DIARIAMENT
with tomato,
onion 5.40€
gourmet
or rocket & assorted
sprouts 2.20€

PULLED PORK BURGERS

PREPARATION : **45 minutes**
COOKING TIME : **4½ hours**
(for the meat)

INGREDIENTS

Makes 6
- 6 plain buns (see recipe on p. 13)
- 2 cloves garlic
- 1 onion
- 1 tsp (2.5 g) paprika
- 1 tsp (2.5 g) ground cumin
- scant ⅔ cup (150 g) ketchup (see recipe on p. 16)
- ⅓ cup (75 ml) Worcestershire sauce
- 3 tbsp (45 ml) red wine vinegar
- 3 tbsp (40 g) brown sugar
- 3 tbsp (45 ml) olive oil
- 1¾ lb (800 g) pork shoulder
- ⅓ cup (80 g) mayonnaise (see recipe on p. 16)
- 1½ tbsp (20 g) mild prepared mustard
- 2 sweet pickled gherkins
- 1½ cups (120 g) iceberg or butterhead lettuce, washed and shredded
- salt, milled pepper

≫ Preheat the oven to 275 °F (140 °C).

≫ Peel and thinly slice the garlic and onion.

≫ In a bowl, combine the spices, ketchup, Worcestershire sauce, vinegar, brown sugar, salt, and pepper.

≫ Heat the oil in a casserole and brown the meat for 3 minutes on each side. Add the onion and garlic, and cook over medium heat for 5 minutes. Add the spicy ketchup mixture together with ⅔ cup (150 ml) water. Place the casserole in the oven with its lid on. Cook for 4 hours and 30 minutes, turning the meat every hour and adding a little water as and when necessary.

≫ Mix together the mayonnaise and mustard.

≫ Cut the gherkins into rounds.

≫ Remove the casserole from the oven and allow the meat to rest for 20 minutes. Preheat the broiler.

≫ Cut the buns in half and toast them lightly in the broiler.

≫ Use a fork to pull the meat apart, into shreds.

≫ Spread the mustard mayonnaise over the cut surfaces of the buns. Distribute the lettuce over the base of each, followed by the pulled pork, and finally the sliced gherkins. Close the buns and serve immediately.

PREPARATION : **30 minutes**
COOKING TIME : **20 minutes**

Pork burgers

INGREDIENTS

Makes 6

- 6 plain or Camembert rolls (see recipes on p. 12)
- 1¾–2 lb (800–900 g) ground pork
- 1 ripe Camembert cheese
- 3 tbsp (45 g) mayonnaise (see recipe on p.16)
- 1½ tbsp (20 g) prepared mustard
- 3 tbsp (45 ml) olive oil
- 12 slices Canadian / smoked back bacon
- generous 1 cup (100 g) mesclun salad (salad mix), washed
- salt, milled pepper

≫ Season the meat with salt and pepper. Shape it into 6 burgers, to fit the buns.

≫ Preheat the broiler.

≫ Cut the Camembert into 12 slices, $\frac{1}{5}$–$\frac{1}{3}$ in. (5–7 mm) thick.

≫ In a bowl, mix together the mayonnaise and mustard.

≫ Heat the oil in a skillet and fry the burgers over medium heat for 6–8 minutes on each side. Transfer to a plate, and keep hot. Drain the fat from the skillet and dry-fry the bacon slices for 1–2 minutes on each side.

≫ Cut the rolls in half and toast them lightly in the broiler.

≫ Spread the mustard mayonnaise over the cut surfaces of the buns. Distribute the lettuce over the bases and place a burger on top, followed by 2 slices each of bacon and Camembert. Close the rolls and serve immediately.

Serve these burgers with celeriac rémoulade with grapefruit (see recipe on p. 20).

BURGERS À LA MILANAISE

PREPARATION : **40 minutes**
COOKING TIME : **6 minutes**

INGREDIENTS

Makes 6
- 6 ciabatta rolls (available from your baker)
- 2 eggs
- ¾ cup (100 g) dry bread crumbs
- 7 tbsp (60 g) all-purpose flour
- 6 very thin veal escalopes, about 4½ oz (130 g) each
- 20 basil leaves
- ¼ cup (60 g) mayonnaise (see recipe on p. 16)
- 2 beefsteak tomatoes
- 4 oz (120 g) piece Parmesan
- oil for frying
- generous 1 cup (100 g) arugula, washed
- salt, milled pepper

》 Beat the eggs lightly in a wide dish. Spread the bread crumbs and flour in two other dishes.

》 Season the escalopes with salt and pepper. Coat them with flour, dip them in the egg, then coat them in bread crumbs.

》 Chop the basil leaves. Combine them with the mayonnaise in a bowl.

》 Preheat the broiler.

》 Wash the tomatoes and slice them into thin rounds. Use a vegetable peeler to cut the Parmesan into shavings.

》 Heat the oil in a skillet and fry the escalopes over medium heat for 2—3 minutes on each side. Drain on paper towels. Wrap them in aluminum foil, and keep hot.

》 Cut the rolls in half and toast them lightly in the broiler.

》 Spread the basil mayonnaise over the cut surfaces of the rolls. Distribute the arugula over the base of each and cover with some tomato slices. Top with an escalope (cut in half if too large to fit the roll) and a few Parmesan shavings. Close the rolls and serve immediately.

MERGUEZ BURGERS

PREPARATION : 30 minutes
COOKING TIME : 30 minutes

INGREDIENTS

Makes 6

- 6 sun-dried tomato or plain buns
  (see recipes on p. 13)
- 2 large onions
- 3 tbsp (45 ml) vegetable oil
- 1½ tbsp (20 g) butter
- 1 tsp (2.5 g) ground cumin
- 1 tsp (5 g) brown sugar
- ½ cup (120 g) ketchup (see recipe
  on p. 16)
- 1 tsp (5 g) harissa paste
- few drops Tabasco Sauce®
- ½ bunch cilantro
- generous 1 cup (100 g)
  butterhead lettuce, washed and
  shredded
- 5½ oz (150 g) Cheddar cheese
- 2 large, ripe tomatoes
- 6 merguez (North African/
  Spanish sausage with red chiles)
- salt, milled pepper

》 Peel and slice the onions. Heat half the oil with the butter in a skillet, and fry the onions over low heat for 20–25 minutes, stirring at regular intervals; halfway through the cooking time, add the cumin, sugar, salt, and pepper.

》 In a bowl, mix half the ketchup with the harissa paste and a few drops of Tabasco®.

》 Chop the cilantro leaves. Mix the chopped cilantro leaves and shredded lettuce together in a bowl.

》 Cut the cheese into 6 equal slices. Wash the tomatoes and slice them into rounds.

》 Preheat the broiler.

》 Heat the remaining oil in a skillet and fry the sausages for 7–10 minutes.

》 Cut the buns in half and toast them lightly in the broiler.

》 Spread the spicy ketchup mixture over the base of each bun and the basic ketchup over the top half. Top with some lettuce and cilantro. Share half the onions between the bases, then add a sausage (cut in half), a slice of cheese, and some tomato rounds to each. Finish with the remaining onions. Close the buns and serve immediately.

PREPARATION : **15 minutes**
COOKING TIME : **5 minutes**

INGREDIENTS

Makes 6

- 6 milk rolls
- 6 lettuce leaves
- 2 tbsp (30 g) butter, melted
- 6 slices ham, $\frac{1}{12}$ inch (2 mm) thick
- ¼ cup (60 g) ketchup (see recipe on p. 16)
- 12 slices processed cheese

KIDS' BURGERS

》 Preheat the oven to 355 °F (180 °C).

》 Wash the lettuce leaves and cut them in half.

》 Line a baking sheet with wax paper. Brush the surface with melted butter.

》 Cut each slice of ham into 3 rectangles. Place these on the wax paper and brush them with melted butter.

》 Cut the rolls in half and place them on another baking sheet.

》 Put both baking sheets in the oven for 5 minutes. Remove from the oven.

》 Spread ketchup over the cut surfaces of the rolls. Place half a lettuce leaf on the base of each. Cover with 3 ham rectangles, 2 cheese slices, and the remaining lettuce leaves. Close the rolls and serve immediately.

FISH
& VEGETABLES

Fish burgers with fries

PREPARATION : **40 minutes**
COOKING TIME : **5 minutes**

INGREDIENTS
Makes 6

For the sauce
- 1 tbsp (8 g) capers
- ½ onion
- 6 small pickled gherkins
- ½ cup (120 g) mayonnaise
  (see recipe on p. 16)
- 1 tbsp (5 g) chopped parsley
- salt, milled pepper

For the burgers
- 6 plain or squid ink buns
  (see recipes on p. 13)
- 2 eggs
- generous $1^2/_3$ cups (200 g)
  all-purpose flour
- 2 pinches baking soda
- $^2/_3$–¾ cup (150–200 ml) beer
- oil for frying
- 6 fillets whiting or pollock, about
  5 oz (140 g) each
- 1½ cups (120 g) butterhead or
  romaine lettuce, washed and
  shredded
- salt, milled pepper

❯ Make the sauce: finely chop the capers and onion. Dice the gherkins. In a bowl, mix the mayonnaise, capers, gherkins, onion, parsley, and season with salt and pepper.

❯ Separate the eggs. In a large bowl, mix the flour with the baking soda, egg yolks, beer, salt, and pepper. Whisk the egg whites and fold them into the batter.

❯ Heat the oil for frying to 340 °F (170 °C).

❯ Cut the fish fillets into pieces if they are too long and use a fork to dip them into the batter. Lower them immediately into the hot oil and fry for 4–5 minutes. Drain on paper towels.

❯ Cut the buns in half. Spread the sauce over the cut surfaces of the buns. Distribute the lettuce over the bases of each, then place the fried fish fillets on top. Close the buns and serve immediately, accompanied by fries.

PREPARATION : **30 minutes**
COOKING TIME : **10 minutes**

THAI-STYLE BURGERS WITH SHRIMP

INGREDIENTS

Makes 6

- 6 plain buns with sesame (see recipe on p. 13)
- 2 red bell peppers
- 2 carrots
- 1 clove garlic
- ½ bunch cilantro
- ¼ cup (60 g) mayonnaise (see recipe on p. 16)
- 1 tbsp (15 g) red curry paste
- 7 tbsp (100 ml) olive oil
- 48 medium raw peeled shrimp
- generous 1 tbsp (10 g) gingerroot powder
- 2 cups (200 g) napa cabbage (Chinese cabbage), washed and shredded
- salt, milled pepper

≫ Peel the bell peppers and carrots, and slice them into thin strips.

≫ Peel and finely chop the garlic. Rinse the cilantro and chop it coarsely.

≫ In a bowl, mix the mayonnaise and half the curry paste.

≫ Heat the olive oil in a large skillet and cook the garlic over low heat for 2 minutes. Add the shrimp, and cook over high heat for 2 minutes. Add the carrots and bell peppers and stir-fry over high heat for 3 minutes. Add the remaining curry paste and the gingerroot. Season with salt and pepper and cook for a further 2 minutes.

≫ Remove from the heat, then add the cilantro and cabbage. Stir well.

≫ Cut the buns in half. Spread the curry mayonnaise over the cut surfaces of each. Place an equal amount of the stir-fry mixture on the base of the buns, allowing 8 shrimp for each. Close the buns and serve immediately.

SALMON BURGERS

PREPARATION : **35 minutes**
COOKING TIME : **5 minutes**

INGREDIENTS
Makes 6
- 6 plain or poppy seed buns
  (see recipe on p. 13)
- 1½ lb (700 g) best-quality
  salmon fillet
- 12 quarters sun-dried tomatoes
  in oil
- 6 sprigs cilantro
- 3½ oz (100 g) piece Parmesan
- 2 cups (500 ml) oil for frying
- 18 large basil leaves
- 3 tbsp (45 ml) olive oil
- 6 tbsp (90 g) béarnaise sauce
  (see recipe on p. 17)
- salt, milled pepper

≫ Preheat the broiler.

≫ Cut the salmon fillet into 12 slices.

≫ Coarsely chop the tomatoes. Remove the cilantro leaves from their stalks. Use a vegetable peeler to cut the Parmesan into shavings.

≫ Heat the oil in a saucepan ready for deep-frying.

≫ When the oil is very hot, add the cilantro and basil leaves and deep-fry for 20–30 seconds. Drain on paper towels. Sprinkle with a little salt.

≫ Heat the olive oil in a skillet and fry the salmon fillets for 1 minute on each side. Season with salt and pepper, and keep hot.

≫ Cut the buns in half and toast them lightly in the broiler.

≫ Spread some béarnaise sauce on the base of each bun. Scatter the sun-dried tomato pieces on top and place 2 pieces of salmon on each bun. Sprinkle the Parmesan shavings and fried herbs over the salmon. Close the buns and serve immediately.

TUNA BURGERS

INGREDIENTS

Makes 6

- 6 plain or squid ink buns
  (see recipes on p. 13)
- 1/3 cup (50 g) capers
- 1/3 cup (80 g) mayonnaise (see
  recipe on p. 16)
- 3 tbsp (45 ml) lemon juice
- 1¼ lb (600 g) bluefin tuna
- 3 tbsp (45 ml) olive oil
- 7 tbsp (100 ml) sweet soy sauce
- 1 yellow bell pepper
- 1 red bell pepper
- 1½ cups (120 g) iceberg or
  romaine lettuce, washed and
  shredded
- salt, milled pepper

≫ Coarsely chop the capers. Mix them in a bowl with the mayonnaise, lemon juice, salt, and pepper.

≫ Season the tuna fillet with salt and pepper. Heat half the olive oil in a skillet and fry the tuna over medium heat for 2 minutes on each side; it should remain pink on the inside. Add the soy sauce to the cooking juices and oil. Spoon the liquid over the fish, turn off the heat, and keep turning the fish in the sauce for 5 minutes. Allow to cool a little.

≫ Seed the bell peppers and cut them into strips. Heat the remaining oil in a skillet and fry the bell peppers over high heat for 2 minutes, to brown lightly.

≫ Slice the tuna.

≫ Cut the buns in half. Spread the caper mayonnaise over the cut surfaces. Distribute the lettuce over the base of each bun, followed by some of the fried bell peppers, and finally the tuna slices. Close the buns and serve immediately.

Serve these burgers with a side of coleslaw with golden raisins (see recipe on p. 21).

Sardine and tapenade burgers

PREPARATION : **30 minutes**
COOKING TIME : **10 minutes**

INGREDIENTS

Makes 6

- 6 sun-dried tomato or plain buns
  (see recipes on p. 13)
- 3 eggs
- salt
- 3 tomatoes
- 1 green bell pepper
- 2 medium onions
- 12 sardines, canned in oil
- ⅔ cup (150 ml) olive oil
- 1 clove garlic
- 6 tbsp (90 g) black tapenade
  (olive paste)

❯ Hard-cook the eggs by boiling them in salted water for 10 minutes. Plunge them into cold water. Peel and slice them into rounds.

❯ Wash the tomatoes and slice them into rounds. Seed the bell pepper and cut it into very thin strips. Peel the onions and slice them into rings.

❯ Drain the sardines.

❯ Preheat the broiler.

❯ Cut the buns in half. Brush the cut surfaces with olive oil and toast them lightly in the broiler.

» Cut the garlic clove in half and rub the cut surfaces over the oiled surfaces of the base and top of each bun. Spread the tapenade over both cut surfaces of the buns.

» Distribute the tomatoes, onions, and hard-cooked egg slices in layers on the base of each bun. Place 2 sardines on top, then some strips of bell pepper. Close the buns and serve immediately.

INGREDIENTS
Makes 6
- 6 plain or poppy seed buns (see recipe on p. 13)
- 3 oz (80 g) piece Parmesan
- 1 bunch chives
- 4 red Belgian endives
- 2 tbsp (30 ml) olive oil
- 2 tbsp (30 ml) cider vinegar
- 9 very fresh eggs
- 2 tbsp (30 g) crème fraîche or heavy sour cream
- salt, milled pepper

BURGERS WITH SCRAMBLED EGGS

》 Use a vegetable peeler to cut the Parmesan into shavings. Wash the chives and snip them into very small pieces.

》 Discard the outer leaves of the Belgian endives and cut out and discard their hard, bitter hearts. Slice the endives finely and mix with the olive oil, vinegar, salt, and pepper in a salad bowl.

》 Break the eggs into the upper part of a double boiler. Season with salt and pepper. Cook the eggs, whisking continuously with a balloon whisk for about 5 minutes, until they have scrambled. Stir in the crème fraîche or sour cream, and then the chives.

》 Cut the buns in half. Distribute the endive salad over the base of each and spoon the scrambled eggs on top. Sprinkle with Parmesan shavings. Close the buns and serve immediately.

BURGERS WITH MOZZARELLA AND BELL PEPPERS

PREPARATION : **30 minutes**
COOKING TIME : **25 minutes**

INGREDIENTS

Makes 6

- 6 ciabatta rolls (available from your baker)
- 1 yellow bell pepper
- 1 red bell pepper
- 1 green bell pepper
- 1 onion
- 3 tbsp (45 ml) olive oil
- 12 pitted green olives
- 6 tbsp (50 g) pine nuts
- generous 1 lb (500 g) smoked mozzarella
- 6 tbsp (90 g) prepared pesto
- generous 1 cup (100 g) arugula, washed
- salt, milled pepper

» Seed the bell peppers and cut them into thin strips. Peel and slice the onion.

» Heat the olive oil in a large skillet and fry the onion for 5 minutes. Add the bell peppers. Season with salt and pepper and cook for 15 minutes, stirring at intervals.

» Meanwhile, chop the olives. Toast the pine nuts in a non-stick skillet, with no oil, for 2–3 minutes.

» When the bell peppers are tender, add the olives and pine nuts. Mix well.

» Preheat the broiler.

» Cut the mozzarella into 6 thick slices. Season with salt and pepper.

》 Cut the rolls in half and toast them lightly in the broiler.

》 Spread the pesto over the cut surfaces of the rolls. Distribute the arugula over the base of each roll, cover with a layer of the bell pepper mixture, and top with a mozzarella slice. Close the rolls and serve immediately.

You could place the assembled burgers in a hot oven for 3-4 minutes, to melt the mozzarella more.

VEGETARIAN BURGERS WITH WALNUTS

PREPARATION : **30 minutes**
COOKING TIME : **10 minutes**

INGREDIENTS

Makes 6

- 6 plain buns with sesame (see recipe on p. 13)
- 2 oz (50 g) walnuts
- 3 oz (80 g) Colby or Cheshire cheese
- 2 carrots
- 1 large zucchini
- 1 bunch chives
- 6 tbsp (90 g) heavy sour cream or soft cream cheese
- 1 cup (100 g) fresh soybean sprouts
- 1/3 cup (75 ml) olive oil
- 6 tofu burgers
- salt, milled pepper

》 Crush the walnuts coarsely. Grate the cheese.

》 Peel the carrot and cut it into thin strips. Wash the zucchini and cut it into thin strips.

》 Chop the chives. Mix them with the sour cream or cream cheese in a bowl, seasoning with salt and pepper.

》 Plunge the soybean sprouts into a saucepan of boiling, salted water to blanch for 2 minutes. Drain and rinse under cold, running water.

》 Heat 3 tablespoons (45 ml) of the olive oil in a wok or skillet and stir-fry the carrot, zucchini, and soybean sprouts over high heat for 3–4 minutes. Season with salt and pepper.

》 Heat the remaining oil in another skillet and fry the tofu burgers for 2–3 minutes on each side. Keep hot.

》 Cut the buns in half. Spread the chive and sour-cream / cream-cheese mixture over the base of each. Place a layer of the vegetables on top, followed by a tofu burger. Sprinkle with grated cheese. Close the buns and serve immediately.

Serve these burgers with a side of rösti (see recipe on p. 20).

HOT DOGS & BAGELS

PREPARATION : **15 minutes**
COOKING TIME : **5 minutes**

INGREDIENTS

Makes 6
- 6 hot dog rolls
- 6 frankfurters
- ¼ cup (60 g) classic yellow prepared mustard
- ¼ cup (60 g) ketchup (see recipe on p. 16)

CLASSIC HOT DOGS

≫ Add the frankfurters to a saucepan of barely simmering water and heat for 5 minutes. Drain.

≫ Cut the rolls open, but do not split them entirely. Transfer to a plate and cover with microwaveable plastic wrap. Heat in a microwave oven for 30 seconds. Alternatively, heat, uncovered, for 2 minutes in a conventional oven.

≫ Place a frankfurter on the base of each roll and drizzle some mustard and ketchup over it. Close and serve immediately.

Serve these hot dogs with a side of homemade fries (see recipe on p. 21).

Chorizo hot dogs

PREPARATION : **30 minutes**
COOKING TIME : **30 minutes**

INGREDIENTS

Makes 6

- 6 individual baguettes
- 3 medium onions
- 1½ tbsp (25 g) butter
- 3 tbsp (45 ml) olive oil
- 11 oz (300 g) large, spicy chorizo
- 5 oz (150 g) Manchego
  (Spanish ewe cheese)
- ¼ cup (60 g) mayonnaise
  (see recipe on p. 16)
- 1 tbsp (8 g) mild chili powder

❯ Peel and slice the onions. Cook them gently in a skillet with the butter and oil over medium heat for 20—25 minutes, until they are golden brown and transparent.

❯ Remove the skin from the chorizo and cut it into very thin slices. Grate the Manchego.

❯ In a bowl, combine the mayonnaise and chili powder.

❯ Preheat the broiler.

❯ Cut the baguettes open, but do not split them entirely. Spread a layer of onions over the lower half and place some sliced chorizo on top. Sprinkle with grated cheese.

❯ Place the baguettes, opened out flat on a baking sheet, in the broiler for a few minutes, to melt and brown the cheese.

❯ Remove from the broiler and spread some chili mayonnaise over the upper cut surface of each baguette. Close and serve immediately.

CHIPO HOT DOGS

PREPARATION : **20 minutes**
COOKING TIME : **30 minutes**

INGREDIENTS

Makes 6
- 6 hot dog rolls
- 1 egg yolk
- 1½ tbsp (20 g) classic yellow
  prepared mustard
- 5–7 tbsp (80–100 ml) vegetable
  oil
- 1 tsp (5 ml) runny honey
- 2 medium onions
- 3 tbsp (45 ml) olive oil
- 1 tsp (5 g) sugar
- 3 tbsp (45 ml) sherry vinegar
- 6 large, herby chipolatas
- generous 1 cup (120 g) arugula
- salt, milled pepper

≫ In a bowl, mix the egg yolk with the mustard. Make a mayonnaise by gradually whisking in the vegetable oil in a thin trickle. Season with salt and pepper. Add the honey and a little cold water if necessary, so that the mayonnaise is not too thick.

≫ Peel and slice the onions. Heat half the olive oil in a skillet and cook the onion gently for 15–20 minutes. Add the sugar, vinegar, salt, and pepper. Stir and continue to cook for a further 5 minutes. Keep hot.

≫ Heat the remaining oil in a skillet and fry the chipolatas for 6–10 minutes. Cut them in half.

≫ Cut the rolls open and heat for 1 minute, covered with microwaveable plastic wrap, in a microwave oven (or for 2 minutes, uncovered, in a conventional oven.)

≫ Distribute the arugula over the base of each and place 2 sausage halves and some onions on top. Drizzle with some mustard mayonnaise. Close the buns and serve immediately.

PREPARATION : **20 minutes**
COOKING TIME : **25 minutes**

CHEESY ANDOUILLE HOT DOGS

INGREDIENTS

Makes 6

- 6 hot dog rolls
- 2 medium mild onions
- 2 tbsp (30 g) butter
- ½ dessert apple
- 1 tbsp (15 g) sugar
- 18 slices, $\frac{1}{8}$ inch (3 mm) thick, andouille sausage
- ¾ oz (80 g) Gruyère, grated
- salt, milled pepper

》 Peel and slice the onions. Heat the butter in a skillet and fry the onions over low heat for approximately 10 minutes, or until they are a pale, golden brown.

》 Peel, halve, and dice the apple. Add to the onions, together with the sugar, salt, and pepper. Cook over low heat for a further 8–10 minutes.

》 Remove the skin from the andouille sausage slices and cut each slice in half.

》 Preheat the broiler.

》 Cut the rolls in half. Spread the onion and apple mixture on the base of each. Add 6 half-slices of sausage to each one, then sprinkle with the grated cheese. Place in the broiler for a few minutes, to melt the cheese.

》 Close the rolls and serve immediately.

Classic yellow mustard could be spread on the cut surfaces of the buns.

MERGUEZ HOT DOGS WITH ONIONS

INGREDIENTS

Makes 6

- 6 hot dog rolls
- 2 large onions
- ¼ cup (60 ml) olive oil
- 1 tsp (2.5 g) ground cumin
- 6 merguez (North African / Spanish sausage with red chiles)
- ¼ cup (60 g) mayonnaise (see recipe on p. 16)
- 1 tbsp (15 g) harissa paste
- juice of ½ lemon
- generous 1 cup (100 g) arugula, washed
- salt, milled pepper

≫ Peel and slice the onions.

≫ Heat 3 tablespoons (45 ml) of the olive oil in a skillet and fry the onions with the cumin over low heat for 20 minutes, until they are transparent and golden brown. Season with salt and pepper.

≫ Heat the remaining olive oil in another skillet and cook the sausages over moderate heat for 5–7 minutes, turning them frequently. (Alternatively, they can be broiled.) Keep hot.

≫ In a bowl, combine the mayonnaise with the harissa paste and lemon juice.

≫ Cut the hot dog rolls open, but do not split them entirely. Heat in a microwave oven for 30 seconds (or for 2 minutes in a conventional oven.)

≫ Spread the harissa mayonnaise over the cut surfaces of each roll. Cover each base with a layer of arugula and then some onions. Add a sausage, close the rolls, and serve immediately.

CHICKEN AND PEANUT HOT DOGS

INGREDIENTS

Makes 6

- 6 hot dog rolls
- 2/3 cup (100 g) peanuts, roasted in their skins and salted
- 2 large onions
- 1½ tbsp (20 g) butter
- 3 tbsp (45 ml) olive oil
- 1 tbsp (15 ml) Tabasco Sauce®
- 18 long, thin slices fillet of chicken breast
- 2½ tbsp (40 ml) runny honey
- 6 tbsp (90 g) chili sauce (see recipe on p. 17)
- 2 cups (150 g) iceberg or romaine lettuce hearts, washed and shredded
- salt, milled pepper

》 Chop the peanuts coarsely. Peel and slice the onions.

》 Heat the butter and half the oil in a skillet and cook the onions over medium heat for 15–20 minutes, until soft. Season with salt and pepper.

》 Stir the Tabasco® into the onions, and transfer them to a plate.

》 Heat the remaining oil in the skillet and fry the sliced chicken fillets for 3–4 minutes on each side. Season with salt and pepper. Add the chopped peanuts and honey. Allow to caramelize over high heat for 2 minutes, stirring continuously.

》 Return the onions to the skillet and keep hot.

》 Cut the rolls open and heat them for 1 minute in a microwave oven (or for 2 minutes in a conventional oven.)

》 Spread the chili sauce on the cut surfaces of each roll. Distribute the lettuce over the base of each and place 3 pieces chicken on top. Finish with the onion and peanut mixture. Close the rolls and serve immediately.

EGG-AND-BACON BAGELS

PREPARATION : **30 minutes**
COOKING TIME : **20 minutes**

INGREDIENTS

Makes 6
- 6 bagels
- 6 eggs
- 1 tbsp (15 ml) vegetable oil
- 12 slices Canadian / smoked back bacon
- 2 sprigs tarragon
- 6 quarters sun-dried tomatoes in oil
- ¼ cup (60 g) mayonnaise (see recipe on p. 16)
- 1½ cups (120 g) butterhead lettuce, washed and shredded
- salt, milled pepper

≫ Hard-cook the eggs in salted, boiling water for 10 minutes. Immerse in a bowl of cold water, then peel them.

≫ Heat the oil in a skillet and fry the bacon over high heat for 5–6 minutes. Drain on paper towels.

≫ Remove the tarragon leaves from their stalks, then chop them. Chop the hard-cooked eggs, tomatoes, and bacon.

≫ In a bowl, mix together the tarragon and mayonnaise. Stir in the chopped eggs, tomatoes, and bacon.

≫ Preheat the broiler (or a toaster).

≫ Cut the bagels in half. Place some lettuce on the base of each and cover with a thick layer of tarragon mayonnaise. Follow with the egg-and-bacon mixture. Close the bagels, pressing the tops gently into place.

≫ Toast the bagels for 4–5 minutes in the broiler / toaster. Serve immediately.

SMOKED SALMON AND CURRY BAGELS

INGREDIENTS

Makes 6
- 6 sesame bagels
- 2 carrots
- 3 tbsp (45 ml) olive oil
- ½ small cucumber
- ½ cup (120 g) heavy sour cream
  or soft cream cheese
- 1 tsp (2.5 g) curry powder
- 1 tsp (5 ml) runny honey
- juice of ½ lemon
- generous 1 lb (500 g) smoked
  salmon
- generous 1 cup (100 g)
  young salad greens (arugula,
  purslane...), washed
- salt, milled pepper

》 Peel and grate the carrots. Mix them in a bowl with half the olive oil, a little salt, and some pepper.

》 Wash the cucumber and slice into thin rounds. Mix these in a bowl with the remaining oil and some salt and pepper.

》 Combine the sour cream / cream cheese in a bowl with the curry powder, honey, and lemon juice. Season with salt and pepper.

》 Have the smoked salmon slices ready to assemble the bagels.

》 Preheat the broiler (or a panini toaster.)

》 Cut the bagels in half. Spread some of the curry mixture on the base of each. Distribute the salad leaves on top, followed by the smoked salmon slices, the grated carrots, and the cucumber slices. Close the bagels, pressing the tops gently into place.

》 Toast the bagels in the broiler (or in a toaster) for 4–5 minutes. Serve immediately.

PREPARATION : **30 minutes**
COOKING TIME : **20 minutes**

INGREDIENTS

Makes 6

- 6 bagels
- ⅓ cup (75 ml) olive oil
- 1¼ lb (600 g) turkey breast slices, each ¾-in (2-cm) thick
- 2 large avocados
- 1 clove garlic
- juice of ½ lemon
- 5½ oz (150 g) piece Colby or Cheshire cheese
- 1½ cups (120 g) butterhead or romaine lettuce
- salt, milled pepper

Bagels with turkey, avocado, and cheese

》 Heat half the olive oil in a skillet and fry the turkey pieces over medium heat for 6–8 minutes on each side. Season with salt and pepper. Keep hot.

》 Peel the avocados and remove the pits. Chop the flesh coarsely and pulse in a blender with the peeled garlic clove, lemon juice, salt, and pepper, to form a smooth purée.

》 Use a vegetable peeler to cut the cheese into shavings.

》 Wash and shred the lettuce. Mix with the remaining oil and some salt and pepper in a salad bowl.

》 Cut the turkey breast slices into thin strips.

》 Preheat the broiler (or a toaster).

》 Cut the bagels in half. Spread some avocado purée on the base of each. Cover with the lettuce and place the turkey pieces on top. Sprinkle with cheese shavings. Close the bagels, pressing the tops gently into place.

》 Toast the bagels in the broiler (or toaster) for 5–7 minutes. Serve immediately.

PREPARATION : **20 minutes**
COOKING TIME : **5 minutes**

INGREDIENTS

Makes 6

- 6 plain or sesame bagels
- 2½ oz (70 g) walnuts
- 11 oz (300 g) semi-soft, ash-coated goat cheese
- 9 oz (250 g) smoked duck breast, thinly sliced
- 1½ cups (120 g) butterhead lettuce, washed and shredded
- 3 tbsp (45 ml) olive oil
- 1½ tbsp (25 ml) runny honey
- milled pepper

DUCK AND GOAT CHEESE BAGELS

》 Chop the walnuts coarsely.

》 Cut the goat cheese into thin slices.

》 Remove any excess fat from the duck breast slices.

》 Preheat the broiler (or a toaster).

》 Cut the bagels in half. Arrange some lettuce on the base of each and sprinkle with half the olive oil. Cover with cheese slices. Drizzle with a little honey, then with the remaining olive oil. Season with milled pepper and sprinkle with chopped walnuts. Finish with duck slices and close the bagels, pressing down gently.

》 Toast the bagels in the broiler (or a toaster) for 4–5 minutes. Serve immediately.

BAGELS PROVENÇAL-STYLE

INGREDIENTS

Makes 6

- 6 plain bagels
- 2 eggs
- 2 large tomatoes
- 1 green bell pepper
- 16 pitted black olives
- 11 oz (300 g) tuna, canned in oil
- 12 anchovy fillets, canned in oil
- 7 tbsp (100 ml) olive oil
- 1½ cups (120 g) butterhead, iceberg, or romaine lettuce, washed and shredded
- salt, milled pepper

》 Hard-cook the eggs by boiling them in salted water for 10 minutes. Plunge them in cold water, then peel them.

》 Plunge the tomatoes into a saucepan of boiling water for 30 seconds. Drain, then rinse them under cold, running water. Skin, seed, and dice them.

》 Seed and dice the bell pepper.

》 Chop the olives, the drained anchovy fillets, and hard-cooked eggs.

》 Combine the drained, flaked tuna in a salad bowl with the anchovies, olives, eggs, tomatoes, and bell pepper. Season with salt, and pepper.

》 Preheat the broiler (or a toaster).

》 Cut the bagels in half. Use a pastry brush to moisten the cut surfaces with a little olive oil. Distribute the lettuce over the base of each and cover with the tuna mixture. Close the bagels, pressing the tops gently into place.

》 Toast the bagels in the broiler (or a toaster) for 4–5 minutes. Serve immediately.

SWEET-AND-SOUR SARDINE BAGELS

PREPARATION : **30 minutes**
COOKING TIME : **15 minutes**

INGREDIENTS

Makes 6

- 6 sesame bagels
- ½ lemon, preserved in salt
- small bunch flat-leaf (Italian) parsley
- 1 large onion
- ⅓ cup (75 ml) olive oil
- generous ½ cup (70 g) pine nuts
- generous ½ cup (70 g) golden raisins
- 12 large sardines, canned in oil
- 2 tbsp (30 ml) runny honey
- generous 1 cup (100 g) arugula, washed
- salt, milled pepper

》 Rinse and wipe the preserved lemon to remove the excess salt. Dice the flesh.

》 Wash and chop the parsley leaves. Peel and finely chop the onion.

》 Sweat the onion in the olive oil over low heat for 5 minutes. Add the pine nuts and cook for 3 minutes. Add the diced lemon, golden raisins, and the coarsely cut, drained sardines. Season with salt and pepper. Stir in the honey and cook for a further 3 minutes. Remove from the heat, then add the chopped parsley. Set aside.

》 Preheat the broiler (or a toaster).

》 Coarsely chop the arugula.

》 Cut the bagels in half. Arrange some arugula on the base of each and cover with the sardine mixture. Close the bagels, pressing down gently.

》 Toast the bagels in the broiler (or toaster) for 5–7 minutes. Serve immediately.

SWEET BURGERS

CHOCOLATE PRALINE WHOOPIE BURGERS

PREPARATION : **45 minutes**
CHILLING TIME : **2 hours**
COOKING TIME : **10—12 minutes**

INGREDIENTS
Makes 12

For the mango jello
- 2 leaves gelatin
- ⅔ cup (150 ml) mango purée

For the filling
- 1¼ cups (200 g) praline chocolate
- ⅔ cup (150 ml) whipping cream

For the "cookie-buns"
- generous ½ cup (120 g) butter, at room temperature
- 9 tbsp (120 g) superfine sugar
- 3 eggs
- 1⅔ cups (230 g) all-purpose flour
- 1 tsp (5 g) baking soda
- 2 tbsp (10 g) orange-flavor chocolate vermicelli
- 2 tbsp (15 g) confectioner's sugar, to dust

》 Make the mango jello: soften the gelatin leaves by soaking them for 10 minutes in a bowl of cold water. Squeeze out the excess moisture and then melt in a saucepan over very low heat. Stir in the mango purée. Spread this mixture on a sheet of plastic wrap placed on a baking sheet. Chill for 2 hours in the refrigerator.

》 Make the filling: chop the chocolate. Bring 3½ tbsp (50 ml) of the whipping cream to a boil in a saucepan. Add the chocolate and stir over very low heat until it has melted. Leave to cool. Whisk the remaining cream until stiff. Gently fold in the chocolate mixture. Chill for 2 hours in the refrigerator.

》 Preheat the oven to 340 °F (170 °C).

》 Make the sweet "cookie-buns:" beat the softened butter and superfine sugar together in a mixing bowl. Beat in the eggs one at a time, and then stir in the flour and baking soda. Make sure the batter is smooth and well blended.

》 Cover one or more baking sheets with non-stick wax paper. Use a pastry bag and large, plain tip to pipe out 24 rounds of the batter 2½—2¾ inches (6—7 cm) in diameter. Sprinkle the surfaces of the cookies with chocolate vermicelli. Place in the oven and bake for 10—12 minutes. Leave to cool.

》 When the mango jello has set, cut it into 12 squares a little larger than the cookies (so that it looks like the cheese in savory burgers).

》 Spread the filling on half the cookies, placing a square of mango jello on top of each one. Cover with the remaining cookies, pressing down gently. Dust with confectioner's sugar, and enjoy!

AMARETTI CITRUS BURGERS

PREPARATION : **30 minutes**
CHILLING TIME : **2 hours**
COOKING TIME : **12 minutes**

INGREDIENTS

Makes 6

For the orange jello
- 2 leaves gelatin
- ⅔ cup (150 ml) fresh orange juice

For the amaretti
- 2 egg whites
- scant 1¼ cups (130 g) confectioner's sugar, + 1 tbsp to dust
- 3 cups (280 g) ground almonds
- 1 tsp (5 ml) almond extract
- grated zest of 1 lime

For the filling
- 11 oz (300 g) Mascarpone
- 6 tbsp (80 g) superfine sugar
- grated zest of 1 lemon
- 1 green apple

≫ Make the jello: soften the gelatin by soaking for 10 minutes in a bowl of cold water. Squeeze out the excess moisture and melt in a saucepan over very low heat. Stir in the orange juice. Line a baking sheet with plastic wrap and pour the orange mixture onto it. Chill for 2 hours in the refrigerator.

≫ Preheat the oven to 350 °F (180 °C).

≫ Make the amaretti: whisk the egg whites in a bowl with the confectioner's sugar and ground almonds. Add the almond extract and grated lime zest. Combine well, to obtain a smooth mixture.

≫ Line a baking sheet with non-stick wax paper and place 6 large balls of almond mixture on it. Press down lightly on the balls, to give them the shape of a burger bun. Place in the oven and bake for 10–12 minutes. Leave to cool.

≫ Make the filling: beat the Mascarpone with the sugar and grated lemon zest. Wash the apple and grate it into a bowl (do not peel it).

≫ When the orange jello has set, cut out 6 squares a little larger than the amaretti "buns" (to look like the slice of cheese in a savory burger).

≫ Carefully cut the amaretti in half. Spread the grated apple and Mascarpone cream on the lower halves. Finish with the orange jello squares. Cover with the top halves of the amaretti "buns." Dust with confectioner's sugar, and enjoy!

CONVERSIONS

LIQUID INGREDIENTS

Metric	American measure	Imperial
5 ml	1 tsp	1 tsp
15 ml	1 tbsp	1 tbsp
35 ml	2½ tbsp	2½ tbsp
60 ml	¼ cup	2 fl oz
125 ml	½ cup	4½ fl oz
250 ml	1 cup	9 fl oz
500 ml	2 cups	17 fl oz
1 liter	4 cups	1 quart

SOLID INGREDIENTS

Metric	American measure	Imperial
30 g	1 oz	1 oz
55 g	2 oz	2 oz
115 g	4 oz	4 oz
170 g	6 oz	6 oz
225 g	8 oz	8 oz
454 g	1 lb	1 lb

OVEN TEMPERATURES

Temperature	° Celsius	° Fahrenheit	Gas mark
Very cool	140 °C	275 °F	1
Cool	150 °C	300 °F	2
Warm	160 °C	325 °F	3
Moderate	180 °C	350 °F	4
Fairly hot	190–200 °C	375–400 °F	5–6
Hot	220 °C	425 °F	7
Very hot	230–240 °C	450–475 °F	8–9

THANKS

Once again, a big thank-you to Barbara and Aurélie at Mango
for this latest addition to a beautiful series.
And to Pierre-Louis, for his lovely photos, and his burger tastings...
with sauce all over his hands!!!
And to my friends Gontran Cherrier, "the" baker of Paris, and Fred,
"the" baker of Montaure in Normandy, for their delicious rolls and buns,
who made it possible for me to create these burgers;
and to Yves Charles for lending me his wonderful knives...
which you can see and buy at www.couteau.com.

It is advisable not to serve dishes that contain raw eggs to very young children, pregnant women, elderly people or to anyone weakened by serious illness. If in any doubt, consult your doctor. Be sure that all the eggs you use are as fresh as possible.

© Mango, Paris - 2013
Original Title: *Burgers! Hot Dogs et Bagels entre Potes*
ISBN 978-23-17001-48-2

Editorial Director: Barbara Sabatier
Editor: Aurélie Cazenave
Graphic Design: Laurent Quellet and Mélissa Chalot
Photoengraving: Amalthéa
Production: Thierry Dubus and Marie Guibert

© for this English edition: h.f.ullmann publishing GmbH

Translation from French: Anna Bennett and Sara Harris in association
with First Edition Translations Ltd, Cambridge, UK
Editing: Sally Heavens in association with First Edition
Translations Ltd, Cambridge, UK
Typesetting: The Write Idea in association with First Edition
Translations Ltd, Cambridge, UK

Project management for h.f.ullmann publishing: Rabea Rittgerodt,
Isabel Weiler

Overall responsibility for production: h.f.ullmann publishing GmbH,
Potsdam, Germany

Printed in Slovenia, 2015

ISBN 978-3-8480-0694-6

10 9 8 7 6 5 4 3 2